It is Written

A Collection of Motivating Verses for the Followers of Christ

Acknowledgments: A number of years ago, Denise Sisco encouraged me to write a book like this—and now it's finally here! Thank you so much for the idea. Additionally, a special thank you to Tom Graham, Richard Morgan, and Jim Styles for their suggestions and feedback on the manuscript.

Cover Design: Jason Robinson 2018

Published in the United States of America 2018

ISBN: 9781730933110

Preface

There are a number of different books that are collections of Bible verses. Perhaps this book could just be added to their ranks.

Nevertheless, this book is different—simply because it is not merely a collection of encouraging verses. Indeed, it *is* a collection of encouraging verses, but at the same time, it is also a collection of verses about subjects that are sometimes seen as academic. It has verses related to the second coming of Jesus Christ, it has verses about the source of evil, and about the oneness of God.

It can be tempting to seek to create a distinction between verses that are encouraging and those that are academic. However, this dichotomy makes it seem as though only *some* verses can truly motivate us and bring about Godly actions. This simply is not the case. Godly doctrine provides a foundation for Godly action—and it is hoped that this book, while providing a collection of motivational verses, can also be a reminder of the importance of doctrine and the way in which it impacts actions.

The book is divided into 42 different sections which have been arranged alphabetically. Each section is introduced by a few words and then composed of at least 5 verses. The book has also been printed in a size that can fit easily into a Bible case, or can simply be carried on its own and read when one has free time. If, in your reading, you come across a verse that you think should have been included in this selection, or even a theme that you feel was left out, please contact me, and I can perhaps include the verse or theme in a future edition.

In the Gospel of John, we are told that the Lord Jesus was the word made flesh. He embodied the words of his Father—and at the same time, those words were constantly on his mind. So many of his actions and his teachings to the crowds reflect the words that were written aforetime. Over and over, he said to the people, "It is written." His mind was filled with Scripture. Just imagine how it would impact your life if you could commit to memory one of the verses in this book every week.

As those who seek to follow the Lord Jesus, it behooves us to also fill our mind with Scripture. As we memorize verses, we give our minds the opportunity to think more as Christ thought. Perhaps this collection of verses can help us to get one step closer to that ideal.

Jason Hensley
2018
jason@speakingofhisglory.com
Further studies at www.thisisyourbible.com

Table of Contents

1 – Anger

There is such a thing as righteous anger (Mark 3:5). Nevertheless, often when we are angry, our anger isn't righteous, or it doesn't inspire us to act righteously. Instead, our anger must be tempered by patience and self-control—because we believe that God is working in all of the circumstances of our lives.

"Rest in the LORD, and wait patiently for him: fret not thyself because of him who prospereth in his way, because of the man who bringeth wicked devices to pass. Cease from anger, and forsake wrath: fret not thyself in any wise to do evil." Psalm 37:7-8

"Be ye angry, and sin not: let not the sun go down upon your wrath." Ephesians 4:26

"Let all bitterness, and wrath, and anger, and clamour, and evil speaking, be put away from you, with all malice: and be ye kind one to another, tenderhearted, forgiving one another, even as God for Christ's sake hath forgiven you." Ephesians 4:31-32

"Wherefore, my beloved brethren, let every man be swift to hear, slow to speak, slow to wrath: for the

wrath of man worketh not the righteousness of God."
James 1:19-20

2 – Anxiety

God is in control. We have peace knowing that indeed, the Judge of all the earth will do right.

"I will both lay me down in peace, and sleep: for thou, LORD, only makest me dwell in safety." Psalm 4:8

"Thou wilt keep him in perfect peace, whose mind is stayed on thee: because he trusteth in thee." Isaiah 26:3

"Peace I leave with you, my peace I give unto you: not as the world giveth, give I unto you. Let not your heart be troubled, neither let it be afraid." John 14:27

"And we know that all things work together for good to them that love God, to them who are the called according to his purpose." Romans 8:28

"Do not be anxious about anything, but in everything by prayer and supplication with thanksgiving let your requests be made known to God. And the peace of God, which surpasses all understanding, will guard your hearts and your minds in Christ Jesus." Philippians 4:6-7 (ESV)

3 - Brotherhood and Unity

A crucial piece of our lives in Christ is our interaction with our fellow believers. They represent the Master to us.

"Then shall the righteous answer him, saying, Lord, when saw we thee an hungred, and fed thee? or thirsty, and gave thee drink? When saw we thee a stranger, and took thee in? or naked, and clothed thee? Or when saw we thee sick, or in prison, and came unto thee? And the King shall answer and say unto them, Verily I say unto you, Inasmuch as ye have done it unto one of the least of these my brethren, ye have done it unto me." Matthew 25:37-40

"Bear ye one another's burdens, and so fulfil the law of Christ." Galatians 6:2

"Do nothing from selfish ambition or conceit, but in humility count others more significant than yourselves. Let each of you look not only to his own interests, but also to the interests of others." Philippians 2:3-4 (ESV)

"Let no one seek his own good, but the good of his neighbor." 1 Corinthians 10:24 (ESV)

"That there should be no schism in the body; but that the members should have the same care one for another. And whether one member suffer, all the members suffer with it; or one member be honoured, all the members rejoice with it." 1 Corinthians 12:25-26

"Remember them that are in bonds, as bound with them; and them which suffer adversity, as being yourselves also in the body." Hebrews 13:3

4 - Children

Our children will see what matters most to us. The Word of God should therefore be on our lips and a constant part of our conversation with them.

"For I know him, that he will command his children and his household after him, and they shall keep the way of the LORD, to do justice and judgment; that the LORD may bring upon Abraham that which he hath spoken of him." Genesis 18:19

"And it shall come to pass, when your children shall say unto you, What mean ye by this service? That ye shall say, It is the sacrifice of the LORD'S passover, who passed over the houses of the children of Israel in Egypt, when he smote the Egyptians, and delivered our houses. And the people bowed the head and worshipped." Exodus 12:26-27

"And these words, which I command thee this day, shall be in thine heart: And thou shalt teach them diligently unto thy children, and shalt talk of them when thou sittest in thine house, and when thou walkest by the way, and when thou liest down, and when thou risest up. And thou shalt bind them for a sign upon thine hand, and they shall be as frontlets between thine eyes. And thou shalt write them upon the posts of thy house, and on thy gates." Deuteronomy 6:6-9

"And, ye fathers, provoke not your children to wrath: but bring them up in the nurture and admonition of the Lord." Ephesians 6:4

"Fathers, provoke not your children to anger, lest they be discouraged." Colossians 3:21

5 - Christ's Return

Though the Lord Jesus departed almost 2000 years ago, it was promised that he would return. His return will herald the resurrection and the kingdom of God.

"But for you who fear my name, the sun of righteousness shall rise with healing in its wings. You shall go out leaping like calves from the stall." Malachi 4:2 (ESV)

"And then shall appear the sign of the Son of man in heaven: and then shall the tribes of the earth mourn, and they shall see the Son of man coming in the clouds of heaven with power and great glory." Matthew 24:30

"Which also said, Ye men of Galilee, why stand ye gazing up into heaven? this same Jesus, which is taken up from you into heaven, shall so come in like manner as ye have seen him go into heaven." Acts 1:11

"For this we declare to you by a word from the Lord, that we who are alive, who are left until the coming of the Lord, will not precede those who have fallen asleep. For the Lord himself will descend from heaven with a cry of command, with the voice of an archangel, and with the sound of the trumpet of God. And the dead in Christ will rise first. Then we who are alive, who are left, will be caught up together with them in the clouds to meet the Lord in the air, and so we will always be with the Lord." 1 Thessalonians 4:15-16 (ESV)

"Behold, he cometh with clouds; and every eye shall see him, and they also which pierced him: and all kindreds of the earth shall wail because of him. Even so, Amen." Revelation 1:7

"And, behold, I come quickly; and my reward is with me, to give every man according as his work shall be." Revelation 22:12

6 - Complaining

Complaining is toxic. It spreads negativity and works against the work of God—because it reveals that we do not accept what God has brought into our lives. Thus, most complaining is ultimately against God Himself (Exodus 16:7; Numbers 16:11).

"And the men, which Moses sent to search the land, who returned, and made all the congregation to murmur against him, by bringing up a slander upon the land, even those men that did bring up the evil report upon the land, died by the plague before the LORD." Numbers 14:36-37

"Now when Jesus was in Bethany, in the house of Simon the leper, there came unto him a woman having an alabaster box of very precious ointment, and poured it on his head, as he sat at meat. But when his disciples saw it, they had indignation, saying, To what purpose is this waste? For this ointment might have been sold for much, and given to the poor. When Jesus understood it, he said unto them, Why trouble ye the woman? for she hath wrought a good work upon me." Matthew 26:6-10

"Neither murmur ye, as some of them also murmured, and were destroyed of the destroyer." 1 Corinthians 10:10

"Do all things without murmurings and disputings." Philippians 2:14

"These are grumblers, malcontents, following their own sinful desires; they are loud-mouthed boasters, showing favoritism to gain advantage." Jude 16 (ESV)

7 - Contentment

Contentment is connected to joy—it is an inner thankfulness for what one has, despite whatever circumstances one might be in. It is an acceptance of what God has provided for us for our good. Contentment is crucial to discipleship.

"Better is little with the fear of the LORD than great treasure and trouble therewith." Proverbs 15:16

"Better is a little with righteousness than great revenues without right." Proverbs 16:8

"And he said unto them, Take heed, and beware of covetousness: for a man's life consisteth not in the abundance of the things which he possesseth." Luke 12:15

"Do all things without murmurings and disputings." Philippians 2:14

"Not that I speak in respect of want: for I have learned, in whatsoever state I am, therewith to be content." Philippians 4:11

"But godliness with contentment is great gain. For we brought nothing into this world, and it is certain we can carry nothing out. And having food and raiment let us be therewith content." 1 Timothy 6:6-8

"Let your conversation be without covetousness; and be content with such things as ye have: for he hath said, I will never leave thee, nor forsake thee." Hebrews 13:5

8 - Dead to Sin

When we are baptized, we put our old lives to death —and just as Christ rose from the dead, when we come out of the water, we are figuratively rising from the death of our old lives. We are new. And just as he was raised and now lives a sinless life, we too are meant to strive to be *dead to sin* and alive to God.

"Likewise reckon ye also yourselves to be dead indeed unto sin, but alive unto God through Jesus Christ our Lord. Let not sin therefore reign in your mortal body, that ye should obey it in the lusts thereof." Romans 6:11-12

"I am crucified with Christ: nevertheless I live; yet not I, but Christ liveth in me: and the life which I now live in the flesh I live by the faith of the Son of God, who loved me, and gave himself for me." Galatians 2:20

"But God forbid that I should glory, save in the cross of our Lord Jesus Christ, by whom the world is crucified unto me, and I unto the world." Galatians 6:14

"If ye then be risen with Christ, seek those things which are above, where Christ sitteth on the right hand of God. Set your affection on things above, not on things on the earth. For ye are dead, and your life is hid with Christ in God. When Christ, who is our life, shall appear, then shall ye also appear with him in glory. Mortify therefore your members which are upon the earth; fornication, uncleanness, inordinate affection, evil concupiscence, and covetousness, which is idolatry." Colossians 3:1-5

"It is a faithful saying: For if we be dead with him, we shall also live with him." 2 Timothy 2:11

"Who his own self bare our sins in his own body on the tree, that we, being dead to sins, should live unto righteousness: by whose stripes ye were healed." 1 Peter 2:24

9 - Deliverance

God watches over His people. He delivers.

Ultimately, He may not deliver from every situation. But the truest and greatest enemy is death—and there is only one way to be saved from it. Despite the fact that death has eventually taken every man and woman, God triumphed over death in raising His son from the grave. We can be part of that deliverance.

"The angel of the LORD encampeth round about them that fear him, and delivereth them." Psalm 34:7

"Because he hath set his love upon me, therefore will I deliver him: I will set him on high, because he hath known my name. He shall call upon me, and I will answer him: I will be with him in trouble; I will deliver him, and honour him." Psalm 91:14-15

"O wretched man that I am! who shall deliver me from the body of this death? I thank God through Jesus Christ our Lord." Romans 7:24-25

"There hath no temptation taken you but such as is common to man: but God is faithful, who will not suffer you to be tempted above that ye are able; but will with the temptation also make a way of escape, that ye may be able to bear it." 1 Corinthians 10:13

"But thou hast fully known my doctrine, manner of life, purpose, faith, longsuffering, charity, patience, persecutions, afflictions, which came unto me at Antioch, at Iconium, at Lystra; what persecutions I endured: but out of them all the Lord delivered me." 2 Timothy 3:10-11

10 - Depression

God loves you. And He offers hope. When all seems hopeless and when all seems meaningless, God gives purpose. He offers life and He wants *you* to share that life with others.

"I waited patiently for the LORD; and he inclined unto me, and heard my cry. He brought me up also out of an horrible pit, out of the miry clay, and set my feet upon a rock, and established my goings. And he hath put a new song in my mouth, even praise unto our God: many shall see it, and fear, and shall trust in the LORD." Psalm 40:1-3

"I will say unto God my rock, Why hast thou forgotten me? why go I mourning because of the oppression of the enemy? As with a sword in my bones, mine enemies reproach me; while they say daily unto me, Where is thy God? Why art thou cast down, O my soul? and why art thou disquieted within me? hope thou in God: for I shall yet praise him, who is the health of my countenance, and my God." Psalm 42:9-11

"Hast thou not known? hast thou not heard, that the everlasting God, the LORD, the Creator of the ends of the earth, fainteth not, neither is weary? there is no searching of his understanding. He giveth power to the faint; and to them that have no might he increaseth strength. Even the youths shall faint and be weary, and the young men shall utterly fall: but they that wait upon the LORD shall renew their strength; they shall mount up with wings as eagles; they shall run, and not be weary; and they shall walk, and not faint." Isaiah 40:28-31

"Come unto me, all ye that labour and are heavy laden, and I will give you rest. Take my yoke upon you, and learn of me; for I am meek and lowly in heart: and ye shall find rest unto your souls. For my yoke is easy, and my burden is light." Matthew 11:28-30

"And God shall wipe away all tears from their eyes; and there shall be no more death, neither sorrow, nor crying, neither shall there be any more pain: for the former things are passed away." Revelation 21:4

II – Faith and Trust

God is working. Even when He sometimes feels far away. Trust Him. Though His plan might not be what we expected or what we wanted, it is always for our good. This is the crux of faith.

"Trust in the LORD with all thine heart; and lean not unto thine own understanding. In all thy ways acknowledge him, and he shall direct thy paths." Proverbs 3:5-6

"And the scripture, foreseeing that God would justify the heathen through faith, preached before the gospel unto Abraham, saying, In thee shall all nations be blessed. So then they which be of faith are blessed with faithful Abraham." Galatians 3:8-9

"For by grace are ye saved through faith; and that not of yourselves: it is the gift of God." Ephesians 2:8

"But my God shall supply all your need according to his riches in glory by Christ Jesus." Philippians 4:19

"Casting all your care upon him; for he careth for you." 1 Peter 5:7

12 - Family Life

God created the family structure for a reason: it reflects His relationship with Christ and with us. He puts us in families because He is training us to join His heavenly family forever. We must be involved in our personal families and the lives of fellow believers—our spiritual family—so we will be prepared to join God's family when the Lord Jesus comes.

"God setteth the solitary in families: He bringeth out those which are bound with chains: But the rebellious dwell in a dry land." Psalm 68:6

"Then shall the King say unto them on his right hand, Come, ye blessed of my Father, inherit the kingdom prepared for you from the foundation of the world: For I was an hungred, and ye gave me meat: I was thirsty, and ye gave me drink: I was a stranger, and ye took me in: Naked, and ye clothed me: I was sick, and ye visited me: I was in prison, and ye came unto me. Then shall the righteous answer him, saying, Lord, when saw we thee an hungred, and fed thee? or thirsty, and gave thee drink? When saw we thee a stranger, and took thee in? or naked, and clothed thee? Or when saw we thee sick, or in prison, and came unto thee? And the King shall answer and say unto them, Verily I say unto you, Inasmuch as ye have done it unto one of the least of these my brethren, ye have done it unto me." Matthew 25:34-40

"As we have therefore opportunity, let us do good unto all men, especially unto them who are of the household of faith." Galatians 6:10

"For this reason I bow my knees before the Father, from whom every family in heaven and on earth is named, that according to the riches of his glory he may grant you to be strengthened with power through his Spirit in your inner being, so that Christ may dwell in your hearts through faith—that you, being rooted and grounded in love, may have strength to comprehend with all the saints what is the breadth and length and height and depth, and to know the love of Christ that surpasses knowledge, that you may be filled with all the fullness of God." Ephesians 3:14-19 (ESV)

"But if any provide not for his own, and specially for those of his own house, he hath denied the faith, and is worse than an infidel." 1 Timothy 5:8

13 - Focus

There are a lot of distractions. But only one thing really matters.

"Blessed is the man that walketh not in the counsel of the ungodly, nor standeth in the way of sinners, nor sitteth in the seat of the scornful. But his delight is in the law of the LORD; and in his law doth he meditate day and night." Psalm 1:1-2

"One thing have I desired of the LORD, that will I seek after; that I may dwell in the house of the LORD all the days of my life, to behold the beauty of the LORD, and to enquire in his temple." Psalm 27:4

"O God, my heart is fixed; I will sing and give praise, even with my glory." Psalm 108:1

"Lay not up for yourselves treasures upon earth, where moth and rust doth corrupt, and where thieves break through and steal: but lay up for yourselves treasures in heaven, where neither moth nor rust doth corrupt, and where thieves do not break through nor steal: for where your treasure is, there will your heart be also." Matthew 6:19-21

"Jesus said unto him, Thou shalt love the Lord thy God with all thy heart, and with all thy soul, and with all thy mind. This is the first and great commandment." Matthew 22:37-38

"For to be carnally minded is death; but to be spiritually minded is life and peace." Romans 8:6

"Therefore, my beloved brethren, be ye stedfast, unmoveable, always abounding in the work of the Lord, forasmuch as ye know that your labour is not in vain in the Lord." 1 Corinthians 15:58

"While we look not at the things which are seen, but at the things which are not seen: for the things which are seen are temporal; but the things which are not seen are eternal." 2 Corinthians 4:18

"Brethren, I count not myself to have apprehended: but this one thing I do, forgetting those things which are behind, and reaching forth unto those things which are before, I press toward the mark for the prize of the high calling of God in Christ Jesus." Philippians 3:13-14

"Meditate upon these things; give thyself wholly to them; that thy profiting may appear to all." 1 Timothy 4:15

14 - Forgiveness and Mercy

God forgives even the most egregious of sins. And so we must forgive those who sin against us.

"Blessed is he whose transgression is forgiven, whose sin is covered. Blessed is the man unto whom the LORD imputeth not iniquity, and in whose spirit there is no guile." Psalm 32:1-2

"Have mercy upon me, O God, according to thy lovingkindness: according unto the multitude of thy tender mercies blot out my transgressions. Wash me throughly from mine iniquity, and cleanse me from my sin." Psalm 51:1-2

"And in that day thou shalt say, O LORD, I will praise thee: though thou wast angry with me, thine anger is turned away, and thou comfortedst me." Isaiah 12:1

"Who is a God like unto thee, that pardoneth iniquity, and passeth by the transgression of the remnant of his heritage? he retaineth not his anger for ever, because he delighteth in mercy." Micah 7:19

"Therefore is the kingdom of heaven likened unto a certain king, which would take account of his servants. And when he had begun to reckon, one was brought unto him, which owed him ten thousand talents. But forasmuch as he had not to pay, his lord commanded him to be sold, and his wife, and children, and all that he had, and payment to be made. The servant therefore fell down, and worshipped him, saying, Lord, have patience with me, and I will pay thee all. Then the lord of that servant was moved with compassion, and loosed him, and forgave him the debt." Matthew 18:23-27

"Repent ye therefore, and be converted, that your sins may be blotted out, when the times of refreshing shall come from the presence of the Lord." Acts 3:19

"And be ye kind one to another, tenderhearted, forgiving one another, even as God for Christ's sake hath forgiven you." Ephesians 4:32

15 - Friendship

Friendship can make all the difference in our discipleship. A Godly friend can give strength, even when ours runs out. An ungodly friend can lead us in the wrong direction, and ultimately destroy us.

"A friend loveth at all times, and a brother is born for adversity." Proverbs 17:17

"A man that hath friends must show himself friendly: and there is a friend that sticketh closer than a brother." Proverbs 18:24

"Faithful are the wounds of a friend; but the kisses of an enemy are deceitful." Proverbs 27:6

"Two are better than one; because they have a good reward for their labour. For if they fall, the one will lift up his fellow: but woe to him that is alone when he falleth; for he hath not another to help him up. Again, if two lie together, they can have heat: but how can one be warm alone? And if one prevail against him, two shall withstand him; and a threefold cord is not quickly broken." Ecclesiastes 4:9-12

"Greater love hath no man than this, that a man lay down his life for his friend. Ye are my friends, if ye do whatsoever I command you. Henceforth I call you not servants; for the servant knoweth not what his lord doeth: but I have called you friends; for all things that I have heard of my Father I have made known unto you." John 15:13-15

"I thank my God upon every remembrance of you, always in every prayer of mine for you all making request with joy, for your fellowship in the gospel from the first day until now." Philippians 1:3-5

16 - God's Control over Everything

God rules over everything. Nothing can happen without Him allowing it—and thus, even the tragedies that occur are not the work of a supernatural devil. God Himself claims responsibility. Even in those tragedies, He is working.

"Thus saith the Lord, Behold, I will raise up evil against thee out of thine own house, and I will take thy wives before thine eyes, and give them unto thy neighbour, and he shall lie with thy wives in the sight of this sun." 2 Samuel 12:11

"But he said unto her, Thou speakest as one of the foolish women speaketh. What? shall we receive good at the hand of God, and shall we not receive evil? In all this did not Job sin with his lips." Job 2:10

"In the day of prosperity be joyful, and in the day of adversity consider: God has made the one as well as the other, so that man may not find out anything that will be after him." Ecclesiastes 7:14 (ESV)

"I am the LORD, and there is none else, there is no God beside me: I girded thee, though thou hast not known me: That they may know from the rising of the sun, and from the west, that there is none beside me. I am the LORD, and there is none else. I form the light, and create darkness: I make peace, and create evil: I the LORD do all these things." Isaiah 45:5-7

"And say, Hear ye the word of the LORD, O kings of Judah, and inhabitants of Jerusalem; Thus saith the LORD of hosts, the God of Israel; Behold, I will bring evil upon this place, the which whosoever heareth, his ears shall tingle." Jeremiah 19:3

"Out of the mouth of the most High proceedeth not evil and good?" Lamentations 3:38

"Shall a trumpet be blown in the city, and the people not be afraid? shall there be evil in a city, and the LORD hath not done it?" Amos 3:6

17 – God's Love Toward Us

God's love is not something that is earned. He loves us—His love is offered to everyone. That doesn't mean, however, that everyone in the world will be saved, or that everyone in the world will have a carefree life. Instead, it means that God *wants* everyone in the world to know Him and to be in His kingdom. It's a reciprocal relationship—God offers His love, but will it be accepted and returned?

"The LORD did not set his love upon you, nor choose you, because ye were more in number than any people; for ye were the fewest of all people: But because the LORD loved you, and because he would keep the oath which he had sworn unto your fathers, hath the LORD brought you out with a mighty hand, and redeemed you out of the house of bondmen, from the hand of Pharaoh king of Egypt." Deuteronomy 7:7-8

"For God so loved the world, that he gave his only begotten Son, that whosoever believeth in him should not perish, but have everlasting life." John 3:16

"For while we were still weak, at the right time Christ died for the ungodly. For one will scarcely die for a righteous person—though perhaps for a good person one would dare even to die—but God shows his love for us in that while we were still sinners, Christ died for us." Romans 5:6-8 (ESV)

"Behold, what manner of love the Father hath bestowed upon us, that we should be called the sons of God: therefore the world knoweth us not, because it knew him not." 1 John 3:1

"He that loveth not knoweth not God; for God is love. In this was manifested the love of God toward us, because that God sent his only begotten Son into the world, that we might live through him. Herein is love, not that we loved God, but that he loved us, and sent his Son to be the propitiation for our sins. Beloved, if God so loved us, we ought also to love one another." 1 John 4:8-11

18 – God's Purpose

When God created the world, He had a purpose. Despite Adam and Eve's sin, that purpose could not and would not be stopped. And thus, one day, that purpose will be fulfilled, here, on earth.

"But as truly as I live, all the earth shall be filled with the glory of the LORD." Numbers 14:21

"And blessed be his glorious name for ever: and let the whole earth be filled with his glory; Amen, and Amen." Psalm 72:19

"They shall not hurt nor destroy in all my holy mountain: for the earth shall be full of the knowledge of the LORD, as the waters cover the sea." Isaiah 11:9

"For the earth shall be filled with the knowledge of the glory of the LORD, as the waters cover the sea." Habakkuk 2:14

"I have glorified thee on the earth: I have finished the work which thou gavest me to do." John 17:4

19 - God's Plan for Israel

God loves the land of Israel. And He loves the children of Abraham, Isaac, and Jacob. In fulfillment of His promises, the kingdom of God will be a time in which Jerusalem is exalted, and a new, spiritual Israel becomes one of the chief of the nations.

"I was glad when they said unto me, Let us go into the house of the LORD. Our feet shall stand within thy gates, O Jerusalem. Jerusalem is builded as a city that is compact together: whither the tribes go up, the tribes of the LORD, unto the testimony of Israel, to give thanks unto the name of the LORD. For there are set thrones of judgment, the thrones of the house of David. Pray for the peace of Jerusalem: they shall prosper that love thee. Peace be within thy walls, and prosperity within thy palaces. For my brethren and companions' sakes, I will now say, Peace be within thee. Because of the house of the LORD our God I will seek thy good." Psalm 122

"For the LORD hath chosen Zion; he hath desired it for his habitation. This is my rest for ever: here will I dwell; for I have desired it." Psalm 132:13-14

"And say unto them, Thus saith the Lord GOD; Behold, I will take the children of Israel from among the heathen, whither they be gone, and will gather them on every side, and bring them into their own land: and I will make them one nation in the land upon the mountains of Israel; and one king shall be king to them all: and they shall be no more two nations, neither shall they be divided into two kingdoms any more at all. Neither shall they defile themselves any more with their idols, nor with their detestable things, nor with any of their transgressions: but I will save them out of all their dwellingplaces, wherein they have sinned, and will cleanse them: so shall they be my people, and I will be their God." Ezekiel 37:21-23

"On that day it shall be said to Jerusalem: 'Fear not, O Zion; let not your hands grow weak. The Lord your God is in your midst, a mighty one who will save; he will rejoice over you with gladness; he will quiet you by his love; he will exult over you with loud singing.'" Zephaniah 3:16-17 (ESV)

"And it shall come to pass in that day, that I will seek to destroy all the nations that come against Jerusalem. And I will pour upon the house of David, and upon the inhabitants of Jerusalem, the spirit of grace and of supplications: and they shall look upon me whom they have pierced, and they shall mourn for him, as one mourneth for his only son, and shall be in bitterness for him, as one that is in bitterness for his firstborn." Zechariah 12:9-10

"I say then, Hath God cast away his people? God forbid. For I also am an Israelite, of the seed of Abraham, of the tribe of Benjamin...For I would not, brethren, that ye should be ignorant of this mystery, lest ye should be wise in your own conceits; that blindness in part is happened to Israel, until the fulness of the Gentiles be come in. And so all Israel shall be saved: as it is written, There shall come out of Sion the Deliverer, and shall turn away ungodliness from Jacob: for this is my covenant unto them, when I shall take away their sins." Romans 11:1, 25-27

20 - Humility

Humility is elusive—because it is so contrary to human nature. Nevertheless, humility is an essential characteristic that makes us like Christ, who humbled himself to the point of dying on the cross.

"Only by pride cometh contention: but with the well advised is wisdom." Proverbs 13:10

"Wherefore let him that thinketh he standeth take heed lest he fall." 1 Corinthians 10:12

"But God forbid that I should glory, save in the cross of our Lord Jesus Christ, by whom the world is crucified unto me, and I unto the world." Galatians 6:14

"Do nothing from selfish ambition or conceit, but in humility count others more significant than yourselves." Philippians 2:3 (ESV)

"Likewise, ye younger, submit yourselves unto the elder. Yea, all of you be subject one to another, and be clothed with humility: for God resisteth the proud, and giveth grace to the humble. Humble yourselves therefore under the mighty hand of God, that he may exalt you in due time." 1 Peter 5:5-6

21 - Husbands and Wives

The relationship between a man and his wife is a picture of the way in which the Lord Jesus gave his life for his followers, and the way in which his followers love and support him. That should never be forgotten.

"Nevertheless, to avoid fornication, let every man have his own wife, and let every woman have her own husband. Let the husband render unto the wife due benevolence: and likewise also the wife unto the husband. The wife hath not power of her own body, but the husband: and likewise also the husband hath not power of his own body, but the wife. Defraud ye not one the other, except it be with consent for a time, that ye may give yourselves to fasting and prayer; and come together again, that Satan tempt you not for your incontinency." 1 Corinthians 7:2-5

"Wives, submit yourselves unto your own husbands, as unto the Lord. For the husband is the head of the wife, even as Christ is the head of the church: and he is the saviour of the body. Therefore as the church is subject unto Christ, so let the wives be to their own husbands in every thing. Husbands, love your wives, even as Christ also loved the church, and gave himself for it; that he might sanctify and cleanse it with the washing of water by the word, that he might present it to himself a glorious church, not having spot, or wrinkle, or any such thing; but that it should be holy and without blemish. So ought men to love their wives as their own bodies. He that loveth his wife loveth himself. For no man ever yet hated his own flesh; but nourisheth and cherisheth it, even as the Lord the church." Ephesians 5:22-29

"Wives, submit yourselves unto your own husbands, as it is fit in the Lord. Husbands, love your wives, and be not bitter against them." Colossians 3:18-19

"Likewise, ye wives, be in subjection to your own husbands; that, if any obey not the word, they also may without the word be won by the conversation of the wives; while they behold your chaste conversation coupled with fear. Whose adorning let it not be that outward adorning of plaiting the hair, and of wearing of gold, or of putting on of apparel; but let it be the hidden man of the heart, in that which is not corruptible, even the ornament of a meek and quiet spirit, which is in the sight of God of great price. For after this manner in the old time the holy women also, who trusted in God, adorned themselves, being in subjection unto their own husbands: even as Sara obeyed Abraham, calling him lord: whose daughters ye are, as long as ye do well, and are not afraid with any amazement. Likewise, ye husbands, dwell with them according to knowledge, giving honour unto the wife, as unto the weaker vessel, and as being heirs together of the grace of life; that your prayers be not hindered." 1 Peter 3:1-7

22 - Immortality

Humanity is a dying race. Though some may teach that the soul has immortality, this is a foreign concept to Scripture. Instead, immortality is something that must be *given* by God to the faithful at the resurrection and judgment. At death, we return to dust—with those who were responsible to God awaiting the resurrection.

"In the sweat of thy face shalt thou eat bread, till thou return unto the ground; for out of it wast thou taken: for dust thou art, and unto dust shalt thou return." Genesis 3:19

"Man that is in honour, and understandeth not, Is like the beasts that perish." Psalm 49:20

"For to him that is joined to all the living there is hope: for a living dog is better than a dead lion. 5 For the living know that they shall die: but the dead know not any thing, neither have they any more a reward; for the memory of them is forgotten. 6 Also their love, and their hatred, and their envy, is now perished; neither have they any more a portion for ever in any thing that is done under the sun." Ecclesiastes 9:4-6

"For the grave cannot praise thee, death can not celebrate thee: They that go down into the pit cannot hope for thy truth. The living, the living, he shall praise thee, as I do this day: The father to the children shall make known thy truth." Isaiah 38:18-19

"But because of your hard and impenitent heart you are storing up wrath for yourself on the day of wrath when God's righteous judgment will be revealed. He will render to each one according to his works: to those who by patience in well-doing seek for glory and honor and immortality, he will give eternal life; but for those who are self-seeking and do not obey the truth, but obey unrighteousness, there will be wrath and fury." Romans 2:5-8 (ESV)

"In a moment, in the twinkling of an eye, at the last trump: for the trumpet shall sound, and the dead shall be raised incorruptible, and we shall be changed. For this corruptible must put on incorruption, and this mortal *must* put on immortality. So when this corruptible shall have put on incorruption, and this mortal shall have put on immortality, then shall be brought to pass the saying that is written, Death is swallowed up in victory." 1 Corinthians 15:52-54

23 – Loneliness

When you feel lonely, remember that God is everywhere. And Christ will not leave his people. They know your feelings.

"Yea, though I walk through the valley of the shadow of death, I will fear no evil: for thou art with me; thy rod and thy staff they comfort me." Psalm 23:4

"Whither shall I go from thy spirit? or whither shall I flee from thy presence? If I ascend up into heaven, thou art there: if I make my bed in hell, behold, thou art there. If I take the wings of the morning, and dwell in the uttermost parts of the sea; even there shall thy hand lead me, and thy right hand shall hold me." Psalm 139:7-10

"Who shall separate us from the love of Christ? shall tribulation, or distress, or persecution, or famine, or nakedness, or peril, or sword? As it is written, For thy sake we are killed all the day long; we are accounted as sheep for the slaughter. Nay, in all these things we are more than conquerors through him that loved us. For I am persuaded, that neither death, nor life, nor angels, nor principalities, nor powers, nor things present, nor things to come, nor height, nor depth, nor any other creature, shall be able to separate us from the love of God, which is in Christ Jesus our Lord." Romans 8:35-39

"Let your conversation be without covetousness; and be content with such things as ye have: for he hath said, I will never leave thee, nor forsake thee." Hebrews 13:5

24 - Love for Others

The love demanded by Christ pushes us beyond what we might expect. We are to *love our enemies*. This is the love that Christ himself demonstrated when he gave his life for the world. This isn't a commandment to feel warm and fuzzy about our enemies. Love isn't an emotion—but a way of life.

"But love ye your enemies, and do good, and lend, hoping for nothing again; and your reward shall be great, and ye shall be the children of the Highest: for he is kind unto the unthankful and to the evil." Luke 6:35

"A new commandment I give unto you, That ye love one another; as I have loved you, that ye also love one another." John 13:34

"This is my commandment, That ye love one another, as I have loved you. Greater love hath no man than this, that a man lay down his life for his friends." John 15:12-13

"Love worketh no ill to his neighbour: therefore love is the fulfilling of the law." Romans 13:10

"If I speak in the tongues of men and of angels, but have not love, I am a noisy gong or a clanging cymbal. And if I have prophetic powers, and understand all mysteries and all knowledge, and if I have all faith, so as to remove mountains, but have not love, I am nothing. If I give away all I have, and if I deliver up my body to be burned, but have not love, I gain nothing. Love is patient and kind; love does not envy or boast; it is not arrogant or rude. It does not insist on its own way; it is not irritable or resentful; it does not rejoice at wrongdoing, but rejoices with the truth. Love bears all things, believes all things, hopes all things, endures all things. Love never ends. As for prophecies, they will pass away; as for tongues, they will cease; as for knowledge, it will pass away. For we know in part and we prophesy in part, but when the perfect comes, the partial will pass away. When I was a child, I spoke like a child, I thought like a child, I reasoned like a child. When I became a man, I gave up childish ways. For now we see in a mirror dimly, but then face to face. Now I know in part; then I shall know fully, even as I have been fully known. So now faith, hope, and love abide, these three; but the greatest of these is love." 1 Corinthians 13 (ESV)

25 - Lust

Lust is strong desire. Where it gets us into trouble is when it is a strong desire for something that isn't of faith. These lusts must be replaced with things that are good—with righteousness, faith, love, and peace, as Paul wrote to Timothy.

"For the commandment is a lamp; and the law is light; and reproofs of instruction are the way of life: To keep thee from the evil woman, from the flattery of the tongue of a strange woman. Lust not after her beauty in thine heart; neither let her take thee with her eyelids. For by means of a whorish woman a man is brought to a piece of bread: and the adulteress will hunt for the precious life. Can a man take fire in his bosom, and his clothes not be burned? Can one go upon hot coals, and his feet not be burned? So he that goeth in to his neighbour's wife; whosoever toucheth her shall not be innocent." Proverbs 6:23-29

"Ye have heard that it was said by them of old time, Thou shalt not commit adultery: But I say unto you, That whosoever looketh on a woman to lust after her hath committed adultery with her already in his heart." Matthew 5:27-28

"So flee youthful passions and pursue righteousness, faith, love, and peace, along with those who call on the Lord from a pure heart." 2 Timothy 2:22 (ESV)

"But every man is tempted, when he is drawn away of his own lust, and enticed. Then when lust hath conceived, it bringeth forth sin: and sin, when it is finished, bringeth forth death." James 1:14-15

"Love not the world, neither the things that are in the world. If any man love the world, the love of the Father is not in him. For all that is in the world, the lust of the flesh, and the lust of the eyes, and the pride of life, is not of the Father, but is of the world." 1 John 2:15-16

26 – Our Singular Purpose

The oneness of God has strong implications. When asked about the greatest commandment, the Lord Jesus didn't simply say that it was to love God with all of our hearts—he first stated that God was one and *then* explained that we must love God with all of our hearts. Why? Perhaps because God deserves *all* of our love, all of our hearts, *because* He is one. There is no other God, no other object of worship that deserves our attention. God is one, and therefore, there is only *one* who demands our all. Thus, even all glory that we give to the Lord Jesus Christ is glory that is ultimately ascribed to His Father—as the Creator of Christ and the One of whom the Lord said "My Father is greater than I."

And so, everything that we do should be done for the glory of God.

"And Jesus answered him, The first of all the commandments is, Hear, O Israel; The Lord our God is one Lord: and thou shalt love the Lord thy God with all thy heart, and with all thy soul, and with all thy mind, and with all thy strength: this is the first commandment." Mark 12:29-30

"That all men should honour the Son, even as they honour the Father. He that honoureth not the Son honoureth not the Father which hath sent him." John 5:23

"Whether therefore ye eat, or drink, or whatsoever ye do, do all to the glory of God." 1 Corinthians 10:30

"That at the name of Jesus every knee should bow, of things in heaven, and things in earth, and things under the earth; and that every tongue should confess that Jesus Christ is Lord, to the glory of God the Father." Philippians 2:10-11

"And whatsoever ye do, do it heartily, as to the Lord, and not unto men." Colossians 3:23

"Thou art worthy, O Lord, to receive glory and honour and power: for thou hast created all things, and for thy pleasure they are and were created." Revelation 4:11

27 - Patience

Patience requires us to consider others and their needs. It takes us out of our myopia and opens our eyes to those around us and to God's timeline. We must remember that He is in control and He determines when things will happen. And, it is a crucial part of God's character.

"And the LORD passed by before him, and proclaimed, The LORD, The LORD God, merciful and gracious, longsuffering, and abundant in goodness and truth." Exodus 34:6

"Be still before the LORD and wait patiently for him; fret not yourself over the one who prospers in his way, over the man who carries out evil devices!" Psalm 37:7 (ESV)

"But thou, O Lord, art a God full of compassion, and gracious, longsuffering, and plenteous in mercy and truth." Psalm 86:15

"Love is patient and kind; love does not envy or boast; it is not arrogant." 1 Corinthians 13:4 (ESV)

"With all humility and gentleness, with patience, bearing with one another in love." Ephesians 4:2 (ESV)

"Preach the word; be instant in season, out of season; reprove, rebuke, exhort with all longsuffering and doctrine." 2 Timothy 4:2

28 - Perspective

When we feel broken, we often cannot see out of our circumstances. The world feels so small and so acute. But better things are to come.

"So teach us to number our days, that we may apply our hearts unto wisdom." Psalm 90:12

"Remember now thy Creator in the days of thy youth, while the evil days come not, nor the years draw nigh, when thou shalt say, I have no pleasure in them." Ecclesiastes 12:1

"The voice said, Cry. And he said, What shall I cry? All flesh is grass, and all the goodliness thereof is as the flower of the field: the grass withereth, the flower fadeth: because the spirit of the LORD bloweth upon it: surely the people is grass. The grass withereth, the flower fadeth: but the word of our God shall stand for ever." Isaiah 40:6-8

"For I reckon that the sufferings of this present time are not worthy to be compared with the glory which shall be revealed in us." Romans 8:18

"For our light affliction, which is but for a moment, worketh for us a far more exceeding and eternal weight of glory." 2 Corinthians 4:17

"Seeing then that all these things shall be dissolved, what manner of persons ought ye to be in all holy conversation and godliness?" 2 Peter 3:11

29 - Praise

God is an awesome God. His character and the greatness of His name should be praised *all of the time.*

"I will bless the LORD at all times: his praise shall continually be in my mouth. My soul shall make her boast in the LORD: the humble shall hear thereof, and be glad. O magnify the LORD with me, and let us exalt his name together." Psalm 34:1-3

"And my tongue shall speak of thy righteousness and of thy praise all the day long." Psalm 35:28

"Let my mouth be filled with thy praise and with thy honour all the day." Psalm 71:8

"My tongue also shall talk of thy righteousness all the day long: for they are confounded, for they are brought unto shame, that seek my hurt." Psalm 71:24

"Sing unto the LORD, bless his name; shew forth his salvation from day to day." Psalm 96:2

"After this manner therefore pray ye: Our Father which art in heaven, Hallowed be thy name." Matthew 6:9

30 - Prayer

Prayer is how we communicate with God—and a healthy relationship requires constant and consistent communication.

"Be merciful unto me, O Lord: for I cry unto thee daily." Psalm 86:3

"And it came to pass in those days, that he went out into a mountain to pray, and continued all night in prayer to God." Luke 6:12

"And he spake a parable unto them to this end, that men ought always to pray, and not to faint." Luke 18:1

"There was a certain man in Caesarea called Cornelius, a centurion of the band called the Italian band, a devout man, and one that feared God with all his house, which gave much alms to the people, and prayed to God alway." Acts 10:1-2

"Rejoicing in hope; patient in tribulation; continuing instant in prayer." Romans 12:12

"Pray without ceasing." 1 Thessalonians 5:17

31 - Rejoicing and Joy

Rejoicing is perhaps the outward manifestation of joy. Joy is something deep within that transcends mere emotion. And both rejoicing and joy are expressions to which God has called His people.

"But unto the place which the LORD your God shall choose out of all your tribes to put his name there, even unto his habitation shall ye seek, and thither thou shalt come: And thither ye shall bring your burnt offerings, and your sacrifices, and your tithes, and heave offerings of your hand, and your vows, and your freewill offerings, and the firstlings of your herds and of your flocks: And there ye shall eat before the LORD your God, and ye shall rejoice in all that ye put your hand unto, ye and your households, wherein the LORD thy God hath blessed thee." Deuteronomy 12:5-7

"Moreover all these curses shall come upon thee, and shall pursue thee, and overtake thee, till thou be destroyed; because thou hearkenedst not unto the voice of the LORD thy God, to keep his commandments and his statutes which he commanded thee: and they shall be upon thee for a sign and for a wonder, and upon thy seed for ever.

Because thou servedst not the LORD thy God with joyfulness, and with gladness of heart, for the abundance of all things." Deuteronomy 28:45-47

"Then he said unto them, Go your way, eat the fat, and drink the sweet, and send portions unto them for whom nothing is prepared: for this day is holy unto our Lord: neither be ye sorry; for the joy of the LORD is your strength." Nehemiah 8:10

"But let all those that put their trust in thee rejoice: let them ever shout for joy, because thou defendest them: let them also that love thy name be joyful in thee." Psalm 5:11

"For his anger endureth but a moment; in his favor is life: weeping may endure for a night, but joy cometh in the morning." Psalm 30:5

"Thou hast turned for me my mourning into dancing: thou hast put off my sackcloth, and girded me with gladness." Psalm 30:11

"Rejoice in the Lord always: and again I say, Rejoice." Philippians 4:4

"Rejoice evermore." 1 Thessalonians 5:16

"Whom having not seen, ye love; in whom, though now ye see him not, yet believing, ye rejoice with joy unspeakable and full of glory." 1 Peter 1:8

32 - Resurrection

At the return of the Lord Jesus to the earth, the dead in Christ will be raised. By the grace of God, those who were faithful will be given immortality and will reign with Christ in the kingdom of God. It will be a spectacular, joyful event when so many believers—and many of our loved ones—come back to life.

"And many of them that sleep in the dust of the earth shall awake, some to everlasting life, and some to shame and everlasting contempt. And they that be wise shall shine as the brightness of the firmament; and they that turn many to righteousness as the stars for ever and ever." Daniel 12:2-3

"Marvel not at this: for the hour is coming, in the which all that are in the graves shall hear his voice, and shall come forth; they that have done good, unto the resurrection of life; and they that have done evil, unto the resurrection of damnation." John 5:28-29

"And have hope toward God, which they themselves also allow, that there shall be a resurrection of the dead, both of the just and unjust." Acts 24:15

"Now this I say, brethren, that flesh and blood cannot inherit the kingdom of God; neither doth corruption inherit incorruption. Behold, I shew you a mystery; We shall not all sleep, but we shall all be changed, in a moment, in the twinkling of an eye, at the last trump: for the trumpet shall sound, and the dead shall be raised incorruptible, and we shall be changed. For this corruptible must put on incorruption, and this mortal must put on immortality." 1 Corinthians 15:50-53

"But we do not want you to be uninformed, brothers, about those who are asleep, that you may not grieve as others do who have no hope. For since we believe that Jesus died and rose again, even so, through Jesus, God will bring with him those who have fallen asleep. For this we declare to you by a word from the Lord, that we who are alive, who are left until the coming of the Lord, will not precede those who have fallen asleep. For the Lord himself will descend from heaven with a cry of command, with the voice of an archangel, and with the sound of the trumpet of God. And the dead in Christ will rise first. Then we who are alive, who are left, will be caught up together with them in the clouds to meet the Lord in the air, and so we will always be with the Lord. Therefore encourage one another with these words." 1 Thessalonians 4:13-18 (ESV)

33 - Self-Control

Controlling our tempers or our instincts can be one of the most challenging things. Nevertheless, those who attempt to keep their minds and bodies from sin are those who are attempting to follow the steps of the Lord—who was tempted and yet did not sin.

"May my heart be blameless in your statutes, that I may not be put to shame!" Psalm 119:80 (ESV)

"He that hath no rule over his own spirit is like a city that is broken down, and without walls." Proverbs 25:28

"Do you not know that in a race all the runners run, but only one receives the prize? So run that you may obtain it. Every athlete exercises self-control in all things. They do it to receive a perishable wreath, but we an imperishable. So I do not run aimlessly; I do not box as one beating the air. But I discipline my body and keep it under control, lest after preaching to others I myself should be disqualified." 1 Corinthians 9:24-27 (ESV)

"For God hath not given us the spirit of fear; but of power, and of love, and of a sound mind." 2 Timothy 1:7

"For this very reason, make every effort to supplement your faith with virtue, and virtue with knowledge, and knowledge with self-control, and self-control with steadfastness, and steadfastness with godliness, and godliness with brotherly affection, and brotherly affection with love. For if these qualities are yours and are increasing, they keep you from being ineffective or unfruitful in the knowledge of our Lord Jesus Christ." 2 Peter 1:5-8 (ESV)

34 - Slander and Gossip

Speaking evil of someone when they have wronged you is simply natural. But God looks for those who bring unity rather than division. He seeks those who use their tongues to build up.

"These six things doth the LORD hate: yea, seven are an abomination unto him...A false witness that speaketh lies, and he that soweth discord among brethren." Proverbs 6:16, 19

"Moreover if thy brother shall trespass against thee, go and tell him his fault between thee and him alone: if he shall hear thee, thou hast gained thy brother. But if he will not hear thee, then take with thee one or two more, that in the mouth of two or three witnesses every word may be established. And if he shall neglect to hear them, tell it unto the church: but if he neglect to hear the church, let him be unto thee as an heathen man and a publican." Matthew 18:15-17

"Let all bitterness, and wrath, and anger, and clamour, and evil speaking, be put away from you, with all malice." Ephesians 4:31

"To speak evil of no one, to avoid quarreling, to be gentle, and to show perfect courtesy toward all people." Titus 3:2 (ESV)

"For he that will love life, and see good days, let him refrain his tongue from evil, and his lips that they speak no guile." 1 Peter 3:10

35 – Strangers and Pilgrims

This life isn't our focus. It isn't about what we acquire, and it isn't about how far we advance in our careers. We are strangers and pilgrims. Just like Christ, whose kingdom was not of this world, we wait for a better day.

"Blessed is the man that walketh not in the counsel of the ungodly, nor standeth in the way of sinners, nor sitteth in the seat of the scornful." Psalm 1:1

"I am a stranger in the earth: hide not thy commandments from me." Psalm 119:19

"They are not of the world, even as I am not of the world." John 17:16

"Jesus answered, My kingdom is not of this world: if my kingdom were of this world, then would my servants fight, that I should not be delivered to the Jews: but now is my kingdom not from hence." John 18:36

"Now then we are ambassadors for Christ, as though God did beseech you by us: we pray you in Christ's stead, be ye reconciled to God." 2 Corinthians 5:20

"Be ye not unequally yoked together with unbelievers: for what fellowship hath righteousness with unrighteousness? and what communion hath light with darkness? And what concord hath Christ with Belial? or what part hath he that believeth with an infidel? And what agreement hath the temple of God with idols? for ye are the temple of the living God; as God hath said, I will dwell in them, and walk in them; and I will be their God, and they shall be my people. Wherefore come out from among them, and be ye separate, saith the Lord, and touch not the unclean thing; and I will receive you. And will be a Father unto you, and ye shall be my sons and daughters, saith the Lord Almighty." 2 Corinthians 6:14-18

"These all died in faith, not having received the promises, but having seen them afar off, and were persuaded of them, and embraced them, and confessed that they were strangers and pilgrims on the earth. For they that say such things declare plainly that they seek a country. And truly, if they had been mindful of that country from whence they came out, they might have had opportunity to have returned. But now they desire a better country, that is, an heavenly: wherefore God is not ashamed to be called their God: for he hath prepared for them a city." Hebrews 11:13-16

"Ye adulterers and adulteresses, know ye not that the friendship of the world is enmity with God? whosoever therefore will be a friend of the world is the enemy of God." James 4:4

"Love not the world, neither the things that are in the world. If any man love the world, the love of the Father is not in him. For all that is in the world, the lust of the flesh, and the lust of the eyes, and the pride of life, is not of the Father, but is of the world. And the world passeth away, and the lust thereof: but he that doeth the will of God abideth for ever." 1 John 2:15-17

36 - Strength

God will give strength to His people. Though they feel weak, through Him they can be strong and endure to the end. Even the greatest enemy—death—can be overcome.

"For by thee I have run through a troop; and by my God have I leaped over a wall." Psalm 18:29

"The LORD is my light and my salvation; whom shall I fear? the LORD is the strength of my life; of whom shall I be afraid?" Psalm 27:1

"Through God we shall do valiantly: for he it is that shall tread down our enemies." Psalm 60:12

"He giveth power to the faint; and to them that have no might he increaseth strength. Even the youths shall faint and be weary, and the young men shall utterly fall: but they that wait upon the LORD shall renew their strength; they shall mount up with wings as eagles; they shall run, and not be weary; and they shall walk, and not faint." Isaiah 40:29-31

"What shall we then say to these things? If God be for us, who can be against us?" Romans 8:31

"I can do all things through Christ which strengtheneth me." Philippians 4:13

37 – Suffering and Trials

Following the Lord Jesus is hard. It will be painful. You will be frustrated. But keep holding on. God *loves you*, and brings suffering in order to *save you* and others.

"The LORD trieth the righteous: but the wicked and him that loveth violence his soul hateth." Psalm 11:5

"Before I was afflicted I went astray: but now have I kept thy word." Psalm 119:67

"It is good for me that I have been afflicted; that I might learn thy statutes." Psalm 119:71

"I know, O LORD, that thy judgments are right, and that thou in faithfulness hast afflicted me." Psalm 119:75

"Sorrow is better than laughter: for by the sadness of the countenance the heart is made better." Ecclesiastes 7:3

"And ye have forgotten the exhortation which speaketh unto you as unto children, My son, despise not thou the chastening of the Lord, nor faint when thou art rebuked of him: for whom the Lord loveth he chasteneth, and scourgeth every son whom he receiveth. If ye endure chastening, God dealeth with you as with sons; for what son is he whom the father chasteneth not?" Hebrews 12:5-7

"Count it all joy, my brothers, when you meet trials of various kinds, for you know that the testing of your faith produces steadfastness. And let steadfastness have its full effect, that you may be perfect and complete, lacking in nothing." James 1:2-4 (ESV)

"That the trial of your faith, being much more precious than of gold that perisheth, though it be tried with fire, might be found unto praise and honour and glory at the appearing of Jesus Christ." 1 Peter 1:7

"Beloved, think it not strange concerning the fiery trial which is to try you, as though some strange thing happened unto you: but rejoice, inasmuch as ye are partakers of Christ's sufferings; that, when his glory shall be revealed, ye may be glad also with exceeding joy." 1 Peter 4:12-13

"As many as I love, I rebuke and chasten: be zealous therefore, and repent." Revelation 3:19

38 - Thankfulness

God has given us so much—and therefore our hearts can abound with thankfulness. Thankfulness is what keeps us from selfishness, anger, and bitterness.

"O LORD, thou hast brought up my soul from the grave: thou hast kept me alive, that I should not go down to the pit. Sing unto the LORD, O ye saints of his, and give thanks at the remembrance of his holiness." Psalm 30:3-4

"Enter into his gates with thanksgiving, and into his courts with praise: be thankful unto him, and bless his name. For the LORD is good; his mercy is everlasting; and his truth endureth to all generations." Psalm 100:4-5

"But thanks be to God, which giveth us the victory through our Lord Jesus Christ." 1 Corinthians 15:57

"Now thanks be unto God, which always causeth us to triumph in Christ, and maketh manifest the savor of his knowledge by us in every place." 2 Corinthians 2:14

"And let the peace of God rule in your hearts, to the which also ye are called in one body; and be ye thankful." Colossians 3:15

"In every thing give thanks: for this is the will of God in Christ Jesus concerning you." 1 Thessalonians 5:18

"And I thank Christ Jesus our Lord, who hath enabled me, for that he counted me faithful, putting me into the ministry." 1 Timothy 1:12

"I exhort therefore, that, first of all, supplications, prayers, intercessions, and giving of thanks, be made for all men; for kings, and for all that are in authority; that we may lead a quiet and peaceable life in all godliness and honesty." 1 Timothy 2:1-2

39 - The Kingdom of God

The hope of the Bible is the kingdom of God on earth. It is in this kingdom that the whole earth will finally be filled with God's glory—when death is destroyed and sorrow and sadness flee away.

"But the meek shall inherit the earth; and shall delight themselves in the abundance of peace." Psalm 37:11

"He shall judge the poor of the people, he shall save the children of the needy, and shall break in pieces the oppressor." Psalm 72:4

"In his days shall the righteous flourish; and abundance of peace so long as the moon endureth. He shall have dominion also from sea to sea, and from the river unto the ends of the earth." Psalm 72:7-8

"The wolf shall dwell with the lamb, and the leopard shall lie down with the young goat, and the calf and the lion and the fattened calf together; and a little child shall lead them. The cow and the bear shall graze; their young shall lie down together; and the lion shall eat straw like the ox." Isaiah 11:6-7 (ESV)

"But in the last days it shall come to pass, that the mountain of the house of the LORD shall be established in the top of the mountains, and it shall be exalted above the hills; and people shall flow unto it. And many nations shall come, and say, Come, and let us go up to the mountain of the LORD, and to the house of the God of Jacob; and he will teach us of his ways, and we will walk in his paths: for the law shall go forth of Zion, and the word of the LORD from Jerusalem. And he shall judge among many people, and rebuke strong nations afar off; and they shall beat their swords into plowshares, and their spears into pruninghooks: nation shall not lift up a sword against nation, neither shall they learn war any more." Micah 4:1-3

"And I heard a great voice out of heaven saying, Behold, the tabernacle of God is with men, and he will dwell with them, and they shall be his people, and God himself shall be with them, and be their God. And God shall wipe away all tears from their eyes; and there shall be no more death, neither sorrow, nor crying, neither shall there be any more pain: for the former things are passed away." Revelation 21:3-4

40 – The Oneness of God

Over and over God emphasizes that He is *one*. He isn't two, He isn't three, He isn't four. He is one sovereign and all-powerful God who is manifested in His son.

"Unto thee it was shewed, that thou mightest know that the LORD he is God; there is none else beside him." Deuteronomy 4:35

"Hear, O Israel: The LORD our God is one LORD. And thou shalt love the LORD thy God with all thine heart, and with all thy soul, and with all thy might." Deuteronomy 6:4-5

"I am the LORD, and there is none else, there is no God beside me: I girded thee, though thou hast not known me: That they may know from the rising of the sun, and from the west, that there is none beside me. I am the LORD, and there is none else." Isaiah 45:5-6

"Ye have heard how I said unto you, I go away, and come again unto you. If ye loved me, ye would rejoice, because I said, I go unto the Father: for my Father is greater than I." John 14:28

"And this is life eternal, that they might know thee the only true God, and Jesus Christ, whom thou hast sent." John 17:3

41 - Truth

Truth matters. It isn't relative. There is one God, and He wants those who claim to follow Him to know who He truly is. Therefore, God's followers must *love Truth* and must continuously look into Scripture to understand Him and His plan.

"And I will delight myself in thy commandments, which I have loved." Psalm 119:47

"Buy the truth, and sell it not; also wisdom, and instruction, and understanding." Proverbs 23:23

"But the hour cometh, and now is, when the true worshippers shall worship the Father in spirit and in truth: for the Father seeketh such to worship him." John 4:23

"Pilate therefore said unto him, Art thou a king then? Jesus answered, Thou sayest that I am a king. To this end was I born, and for this cause came I into the world, that I should bear witness unto the truth. Every one that is of the truth heareth my voice." John 18:37

"I marvel that ye are so soon removed from him that called you into the grace of Christ unto another gospel: which is not another; but there be some that trouble you, and would pervert the gospel of Christ. But though we, or an angel from heaven, preach any other gospel unto you than that which we have preached unto you, let him be accursed. As we said before, so say I now again, if any man preach any other gospel unto you than that ye have received, let him be accursed." Galatians 1:6-9

"One Lord, one faith, one baptism." Ephesians 4:5

"Even him, whose coming is after the working of Satan with all power and signs and lying wonders, and with all deceivableness of unrighteousness in them that perish; because they received not the love of the truth, that they might be saved. And for this cause God shall send them strong delusion, that they should believe a lie: That they all might be damned who believed not the truth, but had pleasure in unrighteousness." 2 Thessalonians 2:9-12

"For the time will come when they will not endure sound doctrine; but after their own lusts shall they heap to themselves teachers, having itching ears; and they shall turn away their ears from the truth, and shall be turned unto fables. But watch thou in all things, endure afflictions, do the work of an evangelist, make full proof of thy ministry." 2 Timothy 4:3-5

"Seeing ye have purified your souls in obeying the truth through the Spirit unto unfeigned love of the brethren, see that ye love one another with a pure heart fervently." 1 Peter 1:22

"I have no greater joy than to hear that my children walk in truth." 3 John 4

42 - Weakness

At times, we can feel completely overwhelmed. We can feel broken. We can feel as though we are failures. And perhaps that's part of what God wants from us—when we are broken, we can realize that it is *Him* that makes us strong, not ourselves. His power is clearly revealed in our weakness.

"Bow down thine ear, O LORD, hear me: for I am poor and needy." Psalm 86:1

"But when Jesus heard that, he said unto them, They that be whole need not a physician, but they that are sick. But go ye and learn what that meaneth, I will have mercy, and not sacrifice: for I am not come to call the righteous, but sinners to repentance." Matthew 9:12-13

"For one will scarcely die for a righteous person— though perhaps for a good person one would dare even to die—but God shows his love for us in that while we were still sinners, Christ died for us." Romans 5:7-8 (ESV)

"But God, being rich in mercy, because of the great love with which he loved us, 5 even when we were dead in our trespasses, made us alive together with Christ—by grace you have been saved." Ephesians 2:4-5 (ESV)

"And he said unto me, My grace is sufficient for thee: for my strength is made perfect in weakness. Most gladly therefore will I rather glory in my infirmities, that the power of Christ may rest upon me." 2 Corinthians 12:9

Appendix - Daily Bible Reading Plan (The Bible Companion)

The Bible Companion was developed by Robert Roberts, a Christadelphian, as a Bible reading plan that takes you through the entire Bible in one year— the Old Testament once and the New Testament twice. The charts below assign approximately four Bible chapters to every day of the year, and break up these chapters into three portions—similar to the way you have three meals each day. Some people like to read a portion around mealtimes; others enjoy reading them all at once.

A number of Christadelphians around the world use the Bible Companion as a structured way to read the Bible every day. Because of that, you can discuss the day's readings with other Bible students who have recently read the same thing. A handy discussion board structured around the Bible Companion can be found at dailyreadings.org.uk.

January

Date	Reading 1	Reading 2	Reading 3
1	Genesis 1, 2	Psalms 1, 2	Matthew 1, 2
2	3, 4	3 - 5	3, 4
3	5, 6	6 - 8	5
4	7, 8	9,10	6
5	9,10	11-13	7
6	11,12	14-16	8
7	13,14	17	9
8	15,16	18	10
9	17,18	19-21	11
10	19	22	12
11	20,21	23-25	13
12	22,23	26-28	14
13	24	29,30	15
14	25,26	31	16
15	27	32	17
16	28,29	33	18
17	30	34	19
18	31	35	20
19	32,33	36	21
20	34,35	37	22
21	36	38	23
22	37	39,40	24
23	38	41-43	25
24	39,40	44	26
25	41	45	27
26	42,43	46-48	28
27	44,45	49	Romans 1, 2
28	46,47	50	3, 4
29	48,50	51,52	5, 6
30	Exodus 1, 2	53-55	7, 8
31	3, 4	56,57	9

February			
Date	Reading 1	Reading 2	Reading 3
1	Exodus 5,6	Psalm 58,59	Romans 10,11
2	7,8	60,61	12
3	9	62,63	13,14
4	10	64,65	15,16
5	11,12	66,67	Mark 1
6	13,14	68	2
7	15	69	3
8	16	70,71	4
9	17,18	72	5
10	19,20	73	6
11	21	74	7
12	22	75,76	8
13	23	77	9
14	24,25	78	10
15	26	79,80	11
16	27	81,82	12
17	28	83,84	13
18	29	85,86	14
19	30	87,88	15,16
20	31,32	89	1 Cor. 1,2
21	33,34	90,91	3
22	35	92,93	4,5
23	36	94,95	6
24	37	96-99	7
25	38	100,101	8,9
26	39,40	102	10
27	Lev. 1,2	103	11
28	3,4	104	12,13

March			
Date	Reading 1	Reading 2	Reading 3
1	Lev. 5,6	Psalms 105	1 Cor. 14
2	7	106	15
3	8	107	16
4	9,10	108,109	2 Cor. 1,2
5	11	110-112	3,4
6	12,13	113,114	5,6,7
7	14	115,116	8,9
8	15	117,118	10,11
9	16	119v1-40	12,13
10	17,18	119v41-80	Luke 1
11	19	119v81-128	2
12	20	119v129-176	3
13	21	120-124	4
14	22	125-127	5
15	23	128-130	6
16	24	131-134	7
17	25	135,136	8
18	26	137-139	9
19	27	140-142	10
20	Numbers 1	143-144	11
21	2	145-147	12
22	3	148-150	13,14
23	4	Proverbs 1	15
24	5	2	16
25	6	3	17
26	7	4	18
27	8,9	5	19
28	10	6	20
29	11	7	21
30	12,13	8,9	22
31	14	10	23

April			
Date	Reading 1	Reading 2	Reading 3
1	Numbers 15	Proverbs 11	Luke 24
2	16	12	Galatians 1,2
3	17,18	13	3,4
4	19	14	5,6
5	20,21	15	Ephes. 1,2
6	22,23	16	3,4
7	24,25	17	5,6
8	26	18	Philip. 1,2
9	27	19	3,4
10	28	20	John 1
11	29,30	21	2,3
12	31	22	4
13	32	23	5
14	33	24	6
15	34	25	7
16	35	26	8
17	36	27	9,10
18	Deut. 1	28	11
19	2	29	12
20	3	30	13,14
21	4	31	15,16
22	5	Eccl. 1	17,18
23	6,7	2	19
24	8,9	3	20,21
25	10,11	4	Acts 1
26	12	5	2
27	13,14	6	3,4
28	15	7	5,6
29	16	8	7
30	17	9	8

May			
Date	Reading 1	Reading 2	Reading 3
1	Deut. 18	Eccl. 10	Acts 9
2	19	11	10
3	20	12	11,12
4	21	Song 1	13
5	22	2	14,15
6	23	3	16,17
7	24	4	18,19
8	25	5	20
9	26	6	21,22
10	27	7	23,24
11	28	8	25,26
12	29	Isaiah 1	27
13	30	2	28
14	31	3,4	Colossians 1
15	32	5	2
16	33,34	6	3,4
17	Joshua 1	7	1 Thess. 1,2
18	2	8	3,4
19	3,4	9	5
20	5,6	10	2 Thess. 1,2
21	7	11	3
22	8	12	1 Tim. 1,2,3
23	9	13	4,5
24	10	14	6
25	11	15	2 Tim. 1
26	12	16	2
27	13	17,18	3,4
28	14	19	Titus 1,2,3
29	15	20,21	Philemon
30	16	22	Hebrews 1,2
31	17	23	3,4,5

June			
Date	Reading 1	Reading 2	Reading 3
1	Joshua 18	Isaiah 24	Hebrews 6,7
2	19	25	8, 9
3	20,21	26,27	10
4	22	28	11
5	23,24	29	12
6	Judges 1	30	13
7	2,3	31	James 1
8	4,5	32	2
9	6	33	3,4
10	7,8	34	5
11	9	35	1 Peter 1
12	10,11	36	2
13	12,13	37	3,4,5
14	14,15	38	2 Peter 1,2
15	16	39	3
16	17,18	40	1 John 1,2
17	19	41	3,4
18	20	42	5
19	21	43	2&3 John
20	Ruth 1,2	44	Jude
21	3,4	45	Rev. 1,2
22	1 Samuel 1	46,47	3,4
23	2	48	5,6
24	3	49	7,8,9
25	4	50	10,11
26	5,6	51	12,13
27	7,8	52	14
28	9	53	15,16
29	10	54	17,18
30	11,12	55	19,20

July			
Date	Reading 1	Reading 2	Reading 3
1	1 Samuel 13	Isaiah 56,57	Rev. 21,22
2	14	58	Matthew 1,2
3	15	59	3,4
4	16	60	5
5	17	61	6
6	18	62	7
7	19	63	8
8	20	64	9
9	21,22	65	10
10	23	66	11
11	24	Jeremiah 1	12
12	25	2	13
13	26,27	3	14
14	28	4	15
15	29,30	5	16
16	31	6	17
17	2 Samuel 1	7	18
18	2	8	19
19	3	9	20
20	4,5	10	21
21	6	11	22
22	7	12	23
23	8,9	13	24
24	10	14	25
25	11	15	26
26	12	16	27
27	13	17	28
28	14	18	Romans 1, 2
29	15	19	3,4
30	16	20	5,6
31	17	21	7,8

August			
Date	Reading 1	Reading 2	Reading 3
1	2 Samuel 18	Jeremiah 22	Romans 9
2	19	23	10,11
3	20,21	24	12
4	22	25	13,14
5	23	26	15,16
6	24	27	Mark 1
7	1 Kings 1	28	2
8	2	29	3
9	3	30	4
10	4, 5	31	5
11	6	32	6
12	7	33	7
13	8	34	8
14	9	35	9
15	10	36	10
16	11	37	11
17	12	38	12
18	13	39	13
19	14	40	14
20	15	41	15
21	16	42	16
22	17	43	1 Cor. 1,2
23	18	44	3
24	19	45,46	4,5
25	20	47	6
26	21	48	7
27	22	49	8,9
28	2 Kings 1,2	50	10
29	3	51	11
30	4	52	12,13
31	5	Lament. 1	14

September			
Date	Reading 1	Reading 2	Reading 3
1	2 Kings 6	Lament. 2	1 Cor. 15
2	7	3	16
3	8	4	2 Cor. 1,2
4	9	5	3,4
5	10	Ezekiel 1	5,6,7
6	11,12	2	8,9
7	13	3	10,11
8	14	4	12,13
9	15	5	Luke 1
10	16	6	2
11	17	7	3
12	18	8	4
13	19	9	5
14	20	10	6
15	21	11	7
16	22,23	12	8
17	24,25	13	9
18	1 Chron. 1	14	10
19	2	15	11
20	3	16	12
21	4	17	13,14
22	5	18	15
23	6	19	16
24	7	20	17
25	8	21	18
26	9	22	19
27	10	23	20
28	11	24	21
29	12	25	22
30	13,14	26	23

October

Date	Reading 1	Reading 2	Reading 3
1	1 Chron. 15	Ezekiel 27	Luke 24
2	16	28	Galatians 1,2
3	17	29	3,4
4	18,19	30	5,6
5	20,21	31	Ephes. 1,2
6	22	32	3,4
7	23	33	5,6
8	24,25	34	Philip. 1,2
9	26	35	3,4
10	27	36	John 1
11	28	37	2,3
12	29	38	4
13	2 Chron. 1,2	39	5
14	3,4	40	6
15	5,6	41	7
16	7	42	8
17	8	43	9,10
18	9	44	11
19	10,11	45	12
20	12,13	46	13,14
21	14,15	47	15,16
22	16,17	48	17,18
23	18,19	Daniel 1	19
24	20	2	20,21
25	21,22	3	Acts 1
26	23	4	2
27	24	5	3,4
28	25	6	5,6
29	26,27	7	7
30	28	8	8
31	29	9	9

November

Date	Reading 1	Reading 2	Reading 3
1	2 Chron. 30	Daniel 10	Acts 10
2	31	11	11,12
3	32	12	13
4	33	Hosea 1	14,15
5	34	2	16,17
6	35	3	18,19
7	36	4	20
8	Ezra 1,2	5	21,22
9	3,4	6	23,24
10	5,6	7	25,26
11	7	8	27
12	8	9	28
13	9	10	Colossians 1
14	10	11	2
15	Nehem. 1,2	12	3,4
16	3	13	1 Thess. 1,2
17	4	14	3,4
18	5,6	Joel 1	5
19	7	2	2 Thess. 1,2
20	8	3	3
21	9	Amos 1	1 Tim. 1,2,3
22	10	2	4,5
23	11	3	6
24	12	4	2 Tim. 1
25	13	5	2
26	Esther 1	6	3,4
27	2	7	Titus 1,2,3
28	3,4	8	Philemon
29	5,6	9	Hebrews 1,2
30	7,8	Obadiah	3,4,5

December			
Date	Reading 1	Reading 2	Reading 3
1	Esther 9,10	Jonah 1	Hebrews 6,7
2	Job 1,2	2,3	8,9
3	3,4	4	10
4	5	Micah 1	11
5	6,7	2	12
6	8	3,4	13
7	9	5	James 1
8	10	6	2
9	11	7	3,4
10	12	Nahum 1,2	5
11	13	3	1 Peter 1
12	14	Habak. 1	2
13	15	2	3,4,5
14	16,17	3	2 Peter 1,2
15	18,19	Zephan. 1	3
16	20	2	1 John 1,2
17	21	3	3,4
18	22	Haggai 1,2	5
19	23,24	Zechariah 1	2&3 John
20	25,26,27	2,3	Jude
21	28	4,5	Rev. 1,2
22	29,30	6,7	3,4
23	31,32	8	5,6
24	33	9	7,8,9
25	34	10	10,11
26	35,36	11	12,13
27	37	12	14
28	38	13,14	15,16
29	39	Malachi 1	17,18
30	40	2	19,20
31	41,42	3,4	21,22

Made in the USA
Columbia, SC
17 October 2024

44540633R00064